Grandfather's Stories From Mexico

Written by Donna Roland
Illustrations by Ron Oden

ISBN 0-941996-09-3

There is a little boy and a little girl who go to school just like you do.

They dress just like you and they play games just like you. They are just like you, but one thing is not the same:

The little boy and girl are from Mexico,
a country which is one of our neighbors.

The little boy's name is Carlos, and the little girl's name is Maria.

Carlos and Maria live in America with their mother and father and their little baby sister in a small brown and yellow house.

Carlos and Maria love the times when their grandfather comes to visit them. They love to hear his stories from their homeland of Mexico.

Grandfather still lives in Mexico, in a small city called Taxco, which is in the mountains.

Taxco is not a big city, but many people who live there are known for making beautiful things. Some are painters, some make things out of the gold and silver that are found nearby.

Grandfather is a silversmith. He makes everything from candlesticks to rings out of silver. The things he makes are very beautiful. Carlos and Maria are very proud of their grandfather.

Grandfather tells them that long ago groups of Indians ruled Mexico. The Indians built large cities and were the first to use a new type of calendar.

Three of the Indian groups, the Mayans, the Toltecs, and the Aztecs, built large stone temples hundreds of years ago. Some of the temples are called pyramids.

The Aztecs were the last Indian group to rule Mexico. They were taken over by soldiers from Spain who wanted the gold and silver riches Mexico had.

The soldiers from Spain brought with them new ideas and a new way of life. The Indians had never seen a horse or a burro before the Spanish soldiers came.

Mexico has learned from the Indians of long ago. They also have learned from the men and women who came there from Spain. The people have pride in their past.

Carlos and Maria have learned many things about their homeland. They have learned about the old ways and how people live in Mexico today.

They know Grandfather lives in the mountains but that Mexico has many kinds of land. Its beaches, deserts, and forests are all part of Mexico.

Grandfather tells Carlos and Maria that
most of the people live in houses made
of stone or clay bricks called adobe.

Like many houses in Mexico, Grandfather's house has a courtyard or patio.
In the middle of it is a beautiful fountain
with bright flowers all around.

The people of Mexico like bright colors.
When there is a party or fiesta,
Grandfather puts on his brightest
clothes. Everyone enjoys a fiesta; it's
a happy time.

Grandfather puts on his best poncho and his sandals, called huaraches. He wears a big hat he calls a sombrero, which is his favorite.

At the fiesta Grandfather hears music being played by a Mariachi Band. There may even be a piñata filled with candy that the boys and girls try to get.

Grandfather also likes going to the bullfights. He tells Carlos and Maria that when the bull runs into the cape, everyone yells "Ole!"

The man who holds the cape is very brave. He is called a matador.

Like most people in Mexico, Grandfather enjoys many things. He enjoys
music, art, fiestas, bullfights, and telling
Carlos and Maria stories. But most of all
he enjoys life.

He often says, "If you want to be happy,
you must enjoy your life the way it has
been given to you." Carlos and Maria
want to enjoy life, just like Grandfather.